The Library of Explorers and Exploration

HENRY HUDSON

English Explorer of the Northwest Passage

Josepha Sherman

the rosen publishing group's
rosen central

Published in 2003 by The Rosen Publishing Group, Inc.
29 East 21st Street, New York, NY 10010

Copyright © 2003 by The Rosen Publishing Group, Inc.

First Edition

Library of Congress Cataloging-in-Publication Data

Sherman, Josepha.
Henry Hudson: English explorer of the Northwest Passage /
Josepha Sherman.
    p. cm. — (The library of explorers and exploration)
Summary: Outlines the events of this English explorer's famous Arctic
journeys and his search for the Northwest Passage to Asia.
Includes bibliographical references and index.
ISBN 0-8239-3620-1 (library binding)
1. Hudson, Henry, d. 1611—Juvenile literature. 2. Explorers—
America—Biography—Juvenile literature. 3. Explorers—Great
Britain—Biography—Juvenile literature. 4. America—Discovery
and exploration—English—Juvenile literature. 5. Northwest
Passage—Discovery and exploration—English—Juvenile literature.
[1. Hudson, Henry, d. 1611. 2. Explorers. 3. America—Discovery
and exploration—English.]
I. Title. II. Series.
E129.H8 S54 2003
910'.92—dc21
                                                    2001008117

Manufactured in the United States of America

CONTENTS

English navigator Henry Hudson explored the extreme polar regions in search of a sea passage to Asia. During his third voyage in 1609 he sailed the waterway now known as the Hudson River and reached Hudson Bay in 1610–1611.

INTRODUCTION

NORTH TO THE ORIENT

Within the chronicles of the age of exploration (roughly 1400–1600), few tales are as romantic as the stories of the Arctic navigators. Unlike the Portuguese explorers, who triumphed during the Middle Ages and Renaissance, navigating newfound trade routes to India, and the Italians, who "discovered" and named the New World, the English Arctic explorers were an unsuccessful clan, a group constantly beset by repeated failure.

John Cabot, for instance, was blocked from continuing in a northwest direction in 1509 by ice and a mutinous crew, while Sir Hugh Willoughby and his group froze to death in frigid waters near Norway during the winter of 1553. John Davis named the eastern coast of Greenland the Land of Desolation during the first of his four failed northern voyages in 1585. Martin Frobisher's consistent failures in the region also discouraged the search for a northern passage to Asia following his third unsuccessful expedition in 1587. Even the

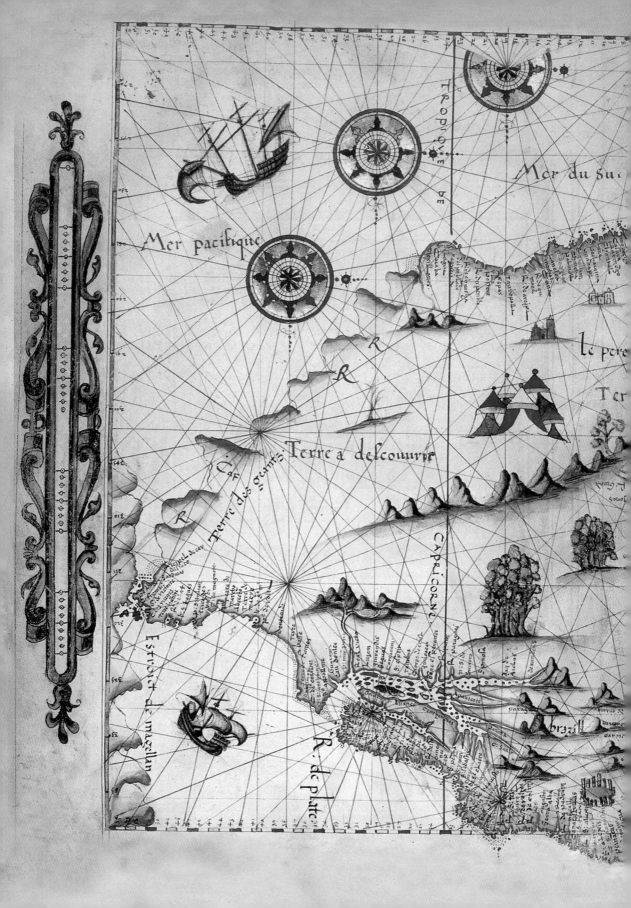

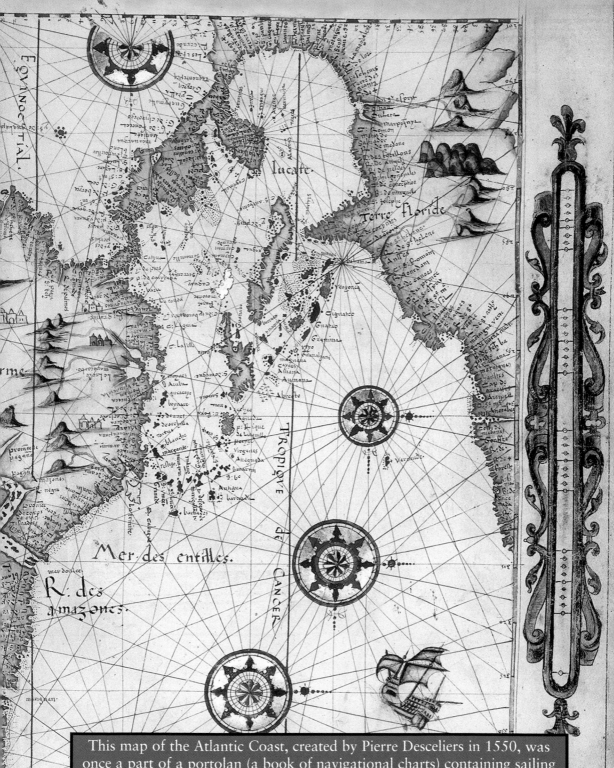

This map of the Atlantic Coast, created by Pierre Desceliers in 1550, was once a part of a portolan (a book of navigational charts) containing sailing directions and guides to coastlines and harbors. Desceliers was a leading mapmaker in his day, part of a School of Cartographers that originated in the port city of Dieppe in the Normandy region of France.

death of William Barents, another explorer who attempted to find a Northwest Passage during his third voyage to the polar region in 1597, did not discourage Henry Hudson. And while their names are scattered throughout the northern Atlantic Ocean—from Frobisher Bay and the Barents Sea, to the Davis Strait and Hudson Bay—their notoriety ends there. None of them captured the elusive northern route to Asia. Still, they are among the most spirited of adventurers because they faced untold challenges.

The maps used by sixteenth- and seventeenth-century navigators—as fantastic as they were factual—provided little information, while the dark seas were clouded by a thick mist and deep fog, so dense in places that guiding a vessel through passing icebergs frequently spelled disaster for many vessels. Moreover, a compass was somewhat unreliable in Arctic waters because of the close proximity of the magnetic North Pole. (The compass needle points farther away from the geographic North Pole by degrees the farther north you travel. This occurs because closest to the poles the earth's lines of magnetic force point downward, causing a compass needle to read inaccurately.) Other aspects of the journey were unsettling, too, such as witnessing what some sailors believed were sea monsters skillfully gliding past their small wooden vessels.

All told, the hardships of sea life—its high death toll, constant confinement, stench of foul odors, disease, bland and inadequate diet, and long hours of maintaining the ship's course and keeping watch—make it clear that the courage needed by sailors was great indeed. The English explorers, like Henry Hudson and his contemporaries who also searched for the northern passage to Asia, were remarkable for braving all of these dangers. They paved the way for the future explorers who mapped most of the northeast portion of North America. They also set the pace for the future of polar exploration that would become so popular in the eighteenth and nineteenth centuries. But this was most true of Hudson, whose last voyage in 1610 inspired the Dutch colonization of America (1624–1664). The Dutch, with their strong desire to profit from the New World, had long-established values that would characterize the nation for centuries afterward.

1

AN AGE OF CURIOSITY

There is one way [left] to discover, which is into the North. For out of Spain they have discovered all the Indies and seas occidental, and out of Portugal all the Indies and seas oriental.
—English merchant Robert Thorne, summarizing the preceding century of exploration in a pamphlet entitled *Thorne's Plan*, 1527

While we know that Henry Hudson explored what would later be called the Hudson River Valley in the name of the Dutch, we also know what he failed to accomplish, and what obsessed him: the search for the Northwest Passage to Asia. And while there aren't many clear facts about the explorer and sea navigator himself, much more information about his life may be drawn from facts about the late sixteenth and early seventeenth centuries, the time in which Hudson lived.

This vista of Ashridge Forest, part of present-day Hertfordshire, England, was the probable birthplace of Henry Hudson. It is a small English village located in the town of Hoddesdon, twenty miles northwest of London.

Hudson was born in England, possibly in the town of Hoddesdon, which is in Hertfordshire County, a few miles northwest of London. Hudson may have been born on September 12, 1570, during the reign of Queen Elizabeth I, in the period known as the Elizabethan Era, although few records from

Elizabethan Record Keeping

Record keeping during the reign of Queen Elizabeth wasn't centralized or controlled. This resulted in a lack of information regarding Henry Hudson's birth, a fairly common condition in that period. Even standardized spelling, which to anyone today seems routine, was inconsistent at the time. William Shakespeare, for instance, who was Hudson's contemporary, spelled his own name several different ways on various documents. There are documented records of numerous spellings, including Shakespeare, Shakespear, Shackspeare, and even Shake-spear.

There was a good reason for the lack of standardized spelling: In the sixteenth century, the majority of people were still unable to read, so rules of spelling were less important than they are today. Once literacy rates rose to include most people, a standardized form of spelling became more relevant so that readers could understand exactly which words they were reading.

this time in history remain regarding Hudson. In fact, scholars aren't even certain of the names of Hudson's parents.

Hudson's family tree provides little more than minor clues about his history. Because there may have been several men who had the first name of "Henry," it's also difficult to understand. Hudson's grandfather, for instance, who was probably a London alderman (councilman), was named Henry Hudson, and there's some evidence that "Henry" might have been Hudson's father's first name as well. Henry the explorer was one of five sons; his brothers were named Christopher, Thomas, John, and Edward.

Unfortunately, personal facts about Henry Hudson are frustratingly few. We're not even sure what Hudson looked like, since the only portraits of him were made long after his death, the date of which is also a mystery; all we know is he disappeared in 1611. We do know that Hudson's family owned a townhouse in London. And since his family was involved in international trade, Hudson must have spent at least some of his early years in that bustling city.

London would have been an exciting place to live. Its crowded cobblestone streets would have been alive with the shouts of merchants and the new plays of William Shakespeare and other dramatists. London's first theater opened in 1576, even though outbreaks of plague often closed public gatherings.

London was heavily and densely populated at the time—a fact that lent itself to the spread of plague and contributed to the estimated 20,000 lives that were lost there to the disease during the sixteenth century. And like many other European cities, London was also buzzing with plans for future exploration and trade.

The four voyages of the Italian explorer Christopher Columbus to the West Indies years before (1492–1504) had proven that there was more to the world than the English had dreamed. After Columbus, John Cabot (1497) and Sir Humphrey Gilbert (1578–1583) had separately explored the coast of North America and claimed land for England. (John Cabot's son Sebastian was actually the first explorer to search for the elusive Northwest Passage for Spain in 1508.) The English seafarer Sir Francis Drake (1577–1580) excited all of England when he became the first English explorer after the Spaniard Ferdinand Magellan (1519–1522) to successfully circumnavigate (travel completely around) the world.

Under the strong leadership of Queen Elizabeth I, England had grown stronger, thriving on trade with the East Indies and Russia. In fact, Hudson's grandfather, the earlier Henry Hudson, was one of the founders of the Muscovy Company, which had made the first contacts with the Russian capital, Moscow, along with Sebastian Cabot.

SEBASTIAN CABOT.

The search for the Northwest Passage was as alluring in Hudson's day as it was when Englishman Sebastian Cabot (above) searched for the great northern waterway to Asia in 1508. Unfortunately, Cabot's story was never verified, as he was considered a boastful fellow. The English halted their search for the elusive passage in order to maintain good relations with Spain, which controlled the area after Columbus claimed it years before.

The young Hudson would almost certainly have been surrounded by talk of adventure and foreign travel. And he would have soon been fascinated by what was to become his lifelong obsession: the search for what would later be officially called the Northwest Passage. This was a conjectured waterway that, so it was hoped, stretched either across the North Pole or (later explorers would hope) across North America to Asia.

The search for the Northwest Passage might sound unusual in today's world, which relies upon modern maps that are accurate to the smallest detail. Even though England had accurate maps of Europe and Asia, neither the Arctic nor the New World had yet been fully mapped. No one had been able to sail to the northernmost regions to see if there was open water or solid land there. Such major rivers as the Saint Lawrence in Canada had been explored, but no one yet knew how far they flowed, or how far inland they could be navigated.

Without a Northwest or Polar Passage, the only way to get to Asia was either by a long, dangerous, and expensive journey east by land, or by a shorter, but certainly just as dangerous, journey by sea. The sea route extended down the African coast, around the Cape of Good Hope (the stormy, treacherous tip of South Africa) then east across the Indian Ocean. The sea journey took months, and between the perils of terrible weather and piracy, many ships never returned. Portugal also had a proprietary claim to this route, another fact that dissuaded exploration of the waters.

The alternate route, which was proved possible by Sir Francis Drake's circling of the world, was longer, more expensive, and even more dangerous. It meant sailing across the Atlantic Ocean, which could take more than six weeks, down around Cape Horn (the storm-racked tip of South America), then out over the Pacific Ocean, which could take twice as long. In short, it would save a great many lives, as well as much money and time, if someone could discover a clear sailing route from England that ran straight across to Asia.

The search for the Northwest Passage was especially important for England since it was fighting an economic battle with the Spanish, the Portuguese, and the Dutch. By providing the country with the safety of a Northwest Passage to Asia, any explorer would drastically improve his country's economic status and expedite direct trade with Asia.

Watching his older brothers and cousins setting out on their journeys, Hudson probably looked forward to his own voyages of exploration. These would have most likely begun in his teens or earlier. Being part of a seafaring family, especially one that made its livelihood from trading, Hudson would have served aboard his family's wooden vessels.

As a young man, Hudson most likely watched many merchant ships sail along the banks of the River Thames and out of London. He was probably enthralled by the beauty of the three-masted ships and their square-rigged sails while he listened to captains talk of their distant voyages.

Sixteenth-century English ships had three masts and carried up to six triangular sails. A ship's prow, or front, would have been a boxy-looking carrack prow, and the stern would have had a raised sterncastle, or two-story cabin. Because they had only wind to power their ships, they would have been utterly dependent on weather conditions to determine speed.

Hudson most likely began his career as a cabin boy, an aide to the ship's captain. He would have learned navigation by cross-staff and compass—sailing by the stars and primary directions. (Although other instruments were also available at the time, such as the astrolabe and the quadrant, most sailors agreed that those were among the most uncertain. This included John Davis, an English seaman who searched for the Northwest Passage in 1585, some years before Hudson did. He wrote about contemporary navigational instruments in his book *Seaman's Secrets*, an account of which is described in a modern book by Samuel Eliot Morison, *The*

The Search for Cathay

The first official expedition to find a shortcut to Asia began in 1576 when Martin Frobisher, a rather flamboyant adventurer and privateer, or licensed pirate, vowed that he would rather face death than return home to England having not reached China, known then as Cathay. He was searching for the Northwest Passage, and made it past Resolution Island, which is part of eastern Arctic Canada, to a bay that turned out to be a dead end. Today it is called Frobisher Bay. It's unlikely that the frustrated explorer would have appreciated the honor. For all his bold words, Frobisher never found what he sought, and the company backing his voyages went bankrupt.

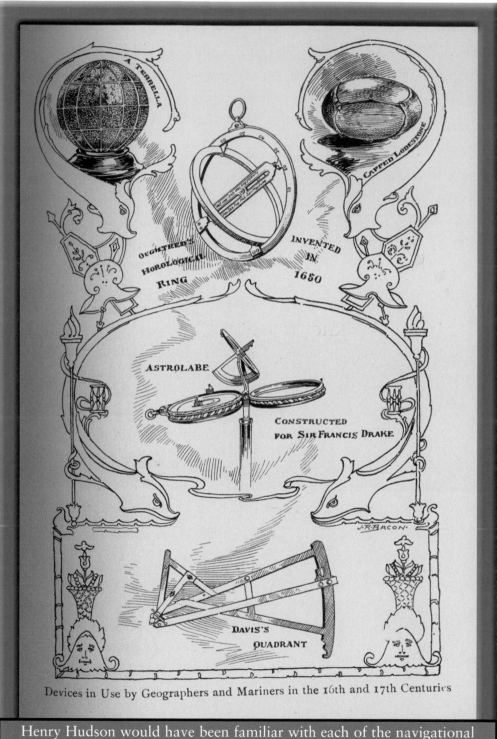

Devices in Use by Geographers and Mariners in the 16th and 17th Centuries

Henry Hudson would have been familiar with each of the navigational instruments shown in this illustration. The astrolabe (center) was built for the English explorer Sir Francis Drake, who circumnavigated the globe in a three-year journey from 1577–1580.

European Discovery of America.) In addition, Hudson would have been skilled at methods of managing sails, cooking, and reading the weather. He was also literate, since he would have been expected to someday captain his own ship and keep its log.

As a teenager, Hudson may have even been part of John Davis's crew in 1587, when the explorer tried his hand at finding the direct route to Asia. Although records of the voyage are frustratingly vague, like the absence of Davis's sailing roster, which keeps us from knowing if Hudson was aboard, we do know that the voyage was planned in Hudson's brother's home. Hudson would have at least heard the plans, if not added to them, and he would have been old enough to sail with Davis.

But Davis's voyage didn't last very long, nor was it successful. In fact, even if Hudson did sail with him, they would have been back in time for Hudson, who was now in his late teens, to help defend his country against the Spanish Armada in 1588. Still, there are no records of Hudson having defended England.

Unfortunately, historians have only scant evidence about what Hudson might have been doing at the end of the sixteenth century. In fact, Hudson's name completely disappears from even the sketchiest of histories until 1607, when it suddenly appears again, this time as an explorer in his own right.

2

ICEBOUND

Anno 1607, April the nineteenth . . . [the Muscovy Company posted notice that] these persons, seamen, purposing to go to sea four days after, for to discover a passage by the North Pole to Cipangu [Japan] and Cathay [China].
— Formal notice given by the Muscovy Company of the sailing of Henry Hudson's ship, the *Hopewell*, 1607

The *Hopewell* (which is, in some accounts, also spelled Hope-well), with Captain Henry Hudson as the leader of the expedition, was put to sea with the goal of finding a northern passage to Asia.

The first recorded mention of Hudson dates back to January 1607, at a meeting of the Muscovy Company's directors, when Reverend Richard Hakluyt, a geographer on the board, had first recommended that he lead the expedition. According to historians, Hakluyt singled Hudson out as a sailor who possessed secret information about the potential passage.

On April 19, 1607, Henry Hudson, his middle son John, and members of his crew attended a special farewell service in the St. Ethelburgh Church in the Bishopsgate section of London.

Richard Hakluyt (1552–1616) was both an ordained English minister and a noted geographer who was fascinated by the topic of exploration, particularly by the English. He wrote several books on the subject including *Principal Navigations*, as well as articles to promote the idea of English colonies in North America.

Historians believe that Hudson's alleged secret information could have been obtained from a pamphlet titled *Thorne's Plan*, written and published by Robert Thorne in 1527, in which he confidently wrote that it would be possible to sail due north, over the North Pole, to Asia.

Modern Travel

Sixteenth-century scientists theorized that the North Pole must be liquid, not solid land or ice. They came to this theory because of their belief that the northernmost Arctic was clear of cloud cover and was warmed by constant sunshine.

Ironically enough, jets today do reach Asia more quickly by the Polar route—but they do it by flying over the undeniably frozen North Pole, a solid mass of icy land once thought to yield an open waterway to Asia.

Hudson, by this point, was married to a woman named Katherine, though her maiden name and the date of their wedding remain unknown. They had three sons—John, Richard, and Oliver—but again, the records pertaining to these events are scarce. We do know that Hudson took John, who was then about fifteen or sixteen years of age, on the voyage with him. All told, the crew on Hudson's first trip numbered between twelve and fifteen.

There was a delay in sailing due to bad weather. But at last, as Hudson himself records in his journal, "The first of May 1607, we wayed [weighed or raised] anchor at Gravesend and were off."

The *Hopewell*, which was a bark—a ship with two main masts and a smaller foremast (front mast)—sailed north by northwest throughout May without Hudson finding anything of note to record, save for the ship's daily position. He also noted a brief alarm on May 30 when the needle on the ship's compass wavered.

That Hudson brushes off so startling an occurrence with only a brief mention hides the fact that there might have been considerable panic aboard the *Hopewell*. After all, this was an age when educated men still firmly believed in demons and ill omens, and something as fixed as a compass suddenly turning unreliable—even briefly—must have been terrifying. It might even have led to the first time that Hudson had to control an attempt at mutiny.

Contrary to the myth that sailors feared it was possible to sail off the edge of the earth, navigators during the age of exploration worried more often that the sea hid great dangers in its depths. They feared sea creatures such as giant squids, super-sized octopi, and great whales like the one shown here.

But the voyage resumed without conflict. By June 11, Hudson sighted six or seven whales near the ship. Whales in that region would have had no reason to fear the *Hopewell*. They might never even have seen a ship. Unfortunately, this was soon to change, when whaling began in earnest only a few years later.

Finally, on June 13, Hudson caught sight of land. It was the coast of Greenland, already known to geographers but not completely mapped. The *Hopewell* sailed up the coast, heading northeast, through the end of June.

Heavy wind, ice, and snow, mixing with unexpected milder patches of warmth and days of blinding fog, marked the voyage. The crew, though somewhat prepared for these conditions with heavier clothing, felt the journey was an unpleasant one. They must have been frightened or just plain miserable, forever damp and chilled. And they must have wondered why Hudson continuously sailed blindly through perilous, unknown waters, when they only wanted to end the voyage.

Sea of Fear

By June 23, to everyone's relief, the weather cleared enough for Hudson to sail northeast from Greenland to what he named "Newland," now known as Spitsbergen in the Svalbard Islands, belonging to Norway. Presumably everyone on board the *Hopewell* was feeling more confident at this point, because up until then, the journey was entirely on open ocean—a fact that gave Hudson great hope about finding the northern sea route to Asia. Because the crew could see where they were going, it's possible that they were sharing some of that hope, too.

But the optimism ended when there turned out to be too much solid ice for the *Hopewell* to continue due north. Instead, Hudson and his men explored what must have seemed to be a confusing mass of islands and icebergs.

27

The northern polar region where Hudson sailed in search of the Northwest Passage is a vast icy ocean surrounded by icebergs of every size, some as large as mountains. Smaller bergs, such as those that move quickly in the wind, are sometimes called growlers. Explorers sail these waters only during the summer months, when navigating is easiest.

The crew's mood improved once more by July 1, when, to everyone's relief, the *Hopewell* reached a large inlet of open water, a rich green place full of seals and walruses. But those high spirits were short-lived. Within the span of ten days, Hudson noted that several members of his crew had become sick after eating spoiled bear meat.

Afterward, they were beset by fog once more. Hudson stated in his journal that a strong wind, or a small gale as he called it, finally delivered the vessel, pushing the *Hopewell* free of fog and ice at the same time. The men's spirits must have been raised when they came to what was to be called Whale Bay, after the many pods of whales they found in it. It is now known as Collins Bay and is situated 750 miles north of the Arctic Circle.

Some of Hudson's crew, led by his first mate, John Colman, were able to land on Northeast Land, the northernmost island of the Svalbard Islands that Hudson and his men were exploring, and were able to hunt game. Fresh meat must have tasted wonderful to men who had been mostly eating salted provisions they'd brought with them. They were also able to refill the ship's casks with freshwater since chunks of ice brought aboard the ship were suitable for drinking; surely this was among the only advantages to northern exploration.

The *Hopewell* was now about 700 miles north of the Arctic Circle and in growing danger of colliding with passing icebergs.

The ship nearly became a casualty when an iceberg almost collided with it, but Hudson quickly steered the *Hopewell* south, and saved everyone.

Hudson accepted the inevitable. It was now the end of August, and the conditions were extremely foggy, wet, and harboring a biting cold. There would be little safe time left for exploration. Rather than risk the lives of his men and himself, he ordered them to continue sailing southward toward England.

"I hoped to have had a free sea between the land and the ice," he wrote in his journal. "This I can assure . . . that by this way there is no passage." But Hudson continued his thought with what seems like a touch of optimism, or maybe an understanding of how commerce would one day make the land more useful: "I think this land may be profitable to those that will adventure it."

Hudson was correct. His reports of the vast numbers of whales in the region profited England, a country that has been linked to the birth of the whaling industry.

On September 15, 1607, the *Hopewell* put into port in Tilbury, England, safe and with a full crew, after a journey through the frozen North that had lasted for three and a half months.

Hudson was home again, but it wouldn't be for long. He had now become a dedicated explorer with a mission: He was hunting for the elusive Northwest Passage to Asia.

3

CHARTING INVISIBLE LANDS

The ninth [day], clear weather . . . We had come a good way northeast. And then we entered into ice . . . the first we saw this voyage. Our hope was to go through it. We stood into it, and held our course . . . until four in the afternoon, at which time we were so far in, and the ice so thick and firm ahead . . . that we had endangered us somewhat too far.

—Journal of Henry Hudson, 1608

When the Muscovy Company heard Henry Hudson's report, they promptly saw the potential for profit. They wanted Hudson to sail back to the region again, this time leading a whaling expedition to Whale Bay.

Hudson refused. He was an explorer, after all, and wasn't interested in becoming a whaling captain. He told the Muscovy Company that just because he hadn't found the passage to Asia on his first voyage of exploration didn't mean it couldn't be found. Throughout the winter of 1607 into 1608, he prepared for his second journey.

Despite repeated requests by the Muscovy Company, Hudson refused to sail solely to guide whaling expeditions. From 1576 to 1625, England led the profitable whaling industry, with the Muscovy Company at the forefront.

Hudson set sail from St. Katherine's docks in London for his second voyage on the *Hopewell*, this time with its planking reinforced as a precaution against ice. It was late April 1608. The funding, once again, came from the Muscovy Company. There was a crew of fifteen on board, including Hudson's son, John, but only three other men who had been on the previous voyage. Evidently, one trip through icy northern waters had been more than enough for most. The three men who did return had faith in Hudson's ability to bring them back safely—and maybe make them rich as well. Everyone understood that there would be a great deal of wealth for anyone who could find the northern passage to Asia.

The Whaling Industry

After Hudson's report of many whales concentrated in a small area became public knowledge, the whaling frenzy began. England and other countries began sending so many ships to the Whale Bay area that it took only a decade or so to nearly exterminate all the whales in the region. Whale fishing lasted well into the twentieth century, only recently becoming challenged by environmentalists.

No one actually laid a formal claim to the Svalbard Islands until the twentieth century, however, when they became Norwegian territory in 1920.

This time on board was Robert Juet, a master seaman and a man of whom Hudson commented in a letter to Hakluyt as being "filled with mean tempers." And while the other members of the crew may have disagreed with the decision to include him, it seems that Juet clearly knew what he was doing because Hudson did sign him on despite his occasionally foul mood.

Bad Omens

At first, the voyage seemed flawless. From April to the end of May, the *Hopewell* sailed north by northeast, reaching the northernmost tip of Norway. Hudson did, however, note in his journal, "[The weather turned] searching cold . . . and then my carpenter was taken sick, and then three or four more of our company were inclining to sickness, I suppose by means of the cold." All apparently recovered, and Hudson makes no further mention of sickness.

Then, on June 9, the voyage almost ended in disaster. Bad weather and colder temperatures nearly lodged the *Hopewell* firmly into a section of ice, but Hudson guided the ship out before it became seriously damaged. He and his crew were able to break free by carefully reversing their course—no easy action with a sailing ship—and backing out, according to his journal, with several minor scrapes of the ship's exterior. After four stressful hours, they had finally broken free.

Afterward, Hudson was more cautious about keeping the *Hopewell* clear of ice, though he noted that the ship's hull again struck something that was probably a small iceberg. Other occurrences were less believable. While the next several days went without incident, Hudson noted in his journal, without any sign of it being unusual, that he and the crew had sighted a mermaid in the icy waters of the Barents Sea.

"Her skin [was] very white, and [she had] long hair hanging down behind, of [the] color black. They saw her tail, which was like the tail of a porpoise, and speckled like a mackerel," according to Hudson's journal.

There have been many theories about what Hudson's men saw, but no clear facts have emerged. Sixteenth-century imaginations were still captured by the magic of the unknown, and traveling in the dark, icy seas—voyages where few had sailed before them—was to travel during an era in which men still believed in magical beings, such as mermaids and sea serpents.

Most explorers during Hudson's time firmly believed, for example, that unicorns could actually be found in Asia. Others were convinced that the deep ocean waters, especially those surrounding the North Pole, were home to strange sea monsters like giant squid, octopuses, and other creatures.

MERMAID.

Although we now know that mermaids are mythical creatures, many sixteenth-century sailors thought they were real. Hudson wrote detailed accounts of mermaid sightings during his voyages, never thinking that he would be doubted.

Other than whale and porpoise sightings, as well as a sea full of "fowls," which was the archaic way of describing fish, there were no other odd descriptions of sights for the remainder of the voyage.

Novaya Zemlya

On June 18, the *Hopewell* came to a barrier of ice on the port, or left side. They had run out of choices. Hudson ordered the ship to sail on to the southeast, and for four days the voyage continued. A week later, Hudson's crew sighted land for the first time. They had reached Nova Zembla, now known as the Russian islands of Novaya Zemlya. Hudson tried to sail north, but the thick ice was too limiting.

Instead, Hudson guided the *Hopewell* due south until it finally reached calm waters. Members of the crew, who probably were relieved, were sent ashore to search the land for anything that would later prove to be valuable, as well as to fill the ship's casks with freshwater. The men returned with news of fertile land, plenty of animal tracks, and, most mysterious of all, reports of two Christian crosses. Since Hudson believed Christians did not inhabit the islands, he must have been puzzled. (It's unlikely that someone who had grown up in predominantly Christian London knew that some pagan peoples also used crosses as symbols.)

But Hudson was more concerned with his obsession to find the northern passage. In doing so, he sent his men to watch for the local walruses on the chance that the animals might have gotten there by warmer currents—currents that would give a clue to the northern route.

But there were no such hints. In July, Hudson wrote that what he had hoped would be a passage between Newland, a place he had discovered on his first voyage, and Novaya Zemlya was blocked with ice. As a result, he decided to head south, hunting for new clues to the location of another passage.

Triumph and Tragedy

That July, the *Hopewell* came upon the mouth of a wide river. Hudson described it in his journal as six to nine miles wide, twenty fathoms (120 feet) deep, with the color and taste of the sea. Its current was also very strong. Could he have found a northern passage at last?

Before Hudson could explore the river, an iceberg swept down on the waves from the north and nearly caught his vessel. The ship had been moored at the time, but it would require hours of shifting wooden beams to block and maneuver the ice around the hull to free it. At last, the *Hopewell* and its crew escaped and were free.

Just fifteen years before Hudson's fourth voyage, the Dutch explorers William Barents and Jacob Heemskerck discovered the Spitsbergen Islands. Barents sailed east to Novaya Zemlya where his ship became trapped in the ice. He and his crew were forced to stay the winter, and built a cabin on shore for warmth (called the Saved House). They were the first expedition to survive an Arctic winter.

NOVA
ZEML

BARENTS SEA

FINLAND

MURMANSK

ARKHANGEL'SK

At that point, the crew collectively decided to return to England, but Hudson was determined to explore the river. To his disappointment, however, it grew more and more shallow. Although he was gravely disappointed, he made careful recordings of all the animal life in the region and added his conclusion that no northern passage was to be found there.

This did not mean that he had abandoned all hope of finding it. In his journal he wrote that he was still inclined to search the area for new options: "Being out of hope to find passage by the northeast . . . my purpose was now to see whether Willoughby's Land is located where it is shown on our charts."

He then gave the order, and the *Hopewell* sailed west by southwest. There was only one problem: Although it showed up on sea charts, including the one used by Hudson, Willoughby's Land, or Willoughby Island, didn't exist. (Even though much of the world was charted by the seventeenth century, mapmakers notoriously added fantasy sketches to their maps, such was the case with what was then known as Willoughby Island.)

Because Willoughby Island was never found, the ever-obsessed Hudson began feeling desperate, yet he remained charged with passion. He planned to do whatever it took to locate the Northwest Passage for England, including sailing to the New World.

Unfortunately, Hudson didn't share his plans with his crew. By August, when they realized that he had no intention of returning home, they were so angry that they were most likely near mutiny.

Because there are no more entries in Hudson's journal until August 7, it is a safe assumption that his crew pressured him to return. Of this, he wrote, "I used all diligence to arrive at London, and therefore now I gave my crew a certificate under my hand, of my free and willing return, without persuasion or force . . ."

His crew had won. Hudson signed this certificate to insure that they wouldn't be in danger of being hanged for attempted mutiny. On August 26, the *Hopewell* again docked in England. Hudson had failed to find any sign of a northern passage, but he was more determined than ever. In fact, he resolved to use any means necessary to find it. Hudson didn't know it yet, but he was going to need all of that determination just to gain another chance.

When he brought the *Hopewell* home to London, it was to a lukewarm reception. The Muscovy Company's directors had learned that he had failed yet again to find a northern passage and were disappointed. They counted all the expenses already spent on the two voyages and flatly turned down his request to finance a third journey.

4

THE PASSAGE TO CATHAY

He shall obtain as much knowledge of the lands as can be done without any considerable loss of time, and . . . deliver over his journals, log–books and charts, together with an account of everything whatsoever which shall happen to him during the voyage without keeping anything back.

— Excerpt from the contract of the Dutch East India Company with Henry Hudson, 1609

Unfortunately, Hudson soon learned that it wasn't merely the Muscovy Company that had lost interest in his struggle to find the Northwest Passage; all of England seemed to have given up on him as well. Suddenly without an employer, Hudson was both worried and frustrated. The Reverend Samuel Purchas, who had gone to see him, wrote, as it was reprinted in Thomas Janvier's *Henry Hudson*, that the English explorer had "sunk into the lowest depth of . . . melancholy [depression], from which no man could rouse him."

In this image, the Half Moon leaves Amsterdam in April 1609, with a crew of twenty Dutch and English sailors. The Half Moon (Halve Maen in Dutch) was commissioned on March 25, 1609, for the Dutch East India Company. She was a ship of exploration and was effectively the spaceship of her age.

Purchas did his best, trying to convince Hudson that the geographic information he'd brought back was a treasure and that by giving it to England he had already gained long-lasting fame. But Hudson wasn't listening.

Then, in November 1608, Hudson unexpectedly received a letter from the Dutch East India Company, a major enterprise in the Netherlands and one that had exclusive rights to Dutch trade in Asia. The directors of the company would pay his expenses if he would come to Amsterdam to meet with them. Hudson must have been suddenly shaken out of his depression. He went to Amsterdam at once and did his best to persuade the company that he could find a successful northern passage. Some believed him, but other members of the board were skeptical. The meeting ended with few results.

Frustrated again, Hudson met with the Dutch geographer Peter Plancius. Plancius also believed in a northern passage and had created a map of the world in 1594 to prove the theory that Asia could be reached by a northern sea route. They exchanged ideas in Latin—the only language they had in common—and struck up a friendship in the process. Hudson also met the engraver Jodocus Hondius, and the two men worked together on Hondius's map of the Arctic.

Hudson receives his commission from officials of the Dutch East India Company. The company was set up on March 20, 1602, by small but ambitious trading businesses tired of losing out on the booming Asian spice trade to the Portuguese. Eventually the Dutch East India Company earned a monopoly over Dutch trade east of Cape Town. The company prospered throughout the seventeenth century and represented a large portion of the Dutch commercial empire in the East Indies. It was dissolved in 1799.

But Hudson's friendships couldn't sponsor him for the third voyage he was seeking. However, a Dutch navigator in Paris told the French king, Henry IV, about Hudson and his ideas. In response, Henry IV sent a secret envoy to meet with Hudson about the future possibility of French exploratory voyages.

This is the Dutch East India House in Amsterdam, home of the Dutch East India Company's headquarters. In addition to offices and warehouses, the company's base of operations contained an auction hall for selling spices.

The Dutch East India Commission

The meeting wasn't as secret as the French might have liked, however, and the Dutch East India Company quickly learned of it, too. They hastily reconsidered their quick denial of Hudson's plan to broaden his search. What, they may have reasoned, if he was correct after all? It made no sense to risk losing the profits that a shortcut to Asia would provide—particularly to one of their national rivals.

It was for this reason that the Dutch signed a contract with Hudson on January 8. In it, Hudson was commissioned by the company to search for another potential northern passage to Asia.

But did the Dutch really trust Hudson? Did they know that he had been secretly communicating with the English captain John Smith about a potential Northwest Passage? Historians believe it's possible, especially since the Dutch signed him on to specifically "think of discovering no other route or passage except the route around the north or northeast above Nova Zembla," according to a special amendment to the 1609 contract between Hudson and the Dutch East India Company.

Hudson's ship, the Half Moon, had an overall height of seventy-eight feet and deck length of just eighty-five feet. It was an awkward vessel, and Hudson requested a different ship for his voyage. The Half Moon was equipped with three masts, four anchors, and six cannons, and could carry eighty tons of cargo.

HALF MOON

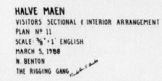

HALVE MAEN
VISITORS SECTIONAL & INTERIOR ARRANGEMENT
PLAN Nº 11
SCALE: ⅜" = 1' ENGLISH
MARCH 5, 1988
N. BENTON
THE RIGGING GANG

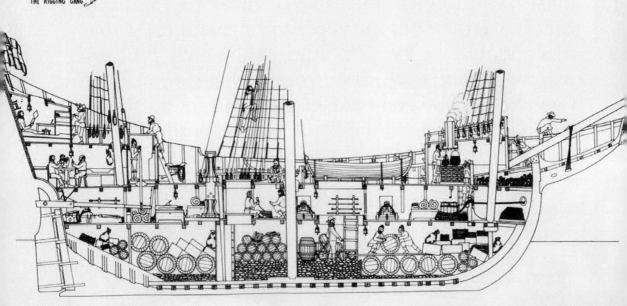

Confusion and Terror

Hudson began preparing for the voyage and signed a crew of twenty people, including, once again, his son John. Ultimately, he gathered a mixed group of sailors, some English, some Dutch. He now had a potential problem since not everyone spoke both languages. It didn't help matters that the English didn't think very highly of the Dutch. The foul-tempered Juet summed up the English sailors' opinions of the Dutch half of the crew with, as it was detailed in his journal, "They are an ugly lot."

It was Juet, in his usual dark mood, who was certain that the Dutch East India Company was deliberately trying to save money by giving Hudson the oldest ship they could find. The vessel was called the *Halve Maen* (the *Half Moon*) and it was admittedly not the most modern of designs. Small and looking like a clumsy version of the *Hopewell*, it rode high in the water. This meant that it would most likely be difficult to handle in rough weather. But the company made it clear that there would be no substitution. In fact, Hudson was told that if he didn't want the *Half Moon*, they would find someone else to captain it.

Hudson accepted the commission. But for whatever reason, he delayed sailing from March 15 to April 6. Only portions of Hudson's journal are still available from his third voyage, since his original writings were the property of

To celebrate the Dutch role in exploring and colonizing America, a replica of Hudson's Half Moon was built at the Snow Dock in Albany, New York, and launched in June of 1989. The Half Moon sails today as a living history exhibit: her cabins and decks are furnished with authentic sea chests, weapons, tools, navigational instruments, and trade goods.

his Dutch employers and were sold at public auction in 1821. And while other writings from that period are available from Juet, Hudson's mate, he used two different forms of calendars while writing it, making the dates uncertain.

With a crew composed of people who didn't understand each other, it was just a matter of time before trouble erupted. Sure enough, quarrels grew commonplace as the *Half Moon* sailed north toward Norway. By mid May, the weather, like the moods of those aboard the ship, had turned foul. Arguments between the English and Dutch crewmen became more frequent. Hudson was hardly in the best of moods, either, since the wind was too strong to allow him to continue sailing north, not even as far as the Russian islands now known as Novaya Zemlya.

We have no way of knowing what happened next. Was it an attempt at mutiny? Was Juet behind the trouble? After nearly two weeks of wind and bad weather, Hudson changed his mind about their intended destination and decided that the time had come to sail in a southerly direction. Perhaps that had been his plan all along, since he had maps on board of the New World. His crew agreed to the change of course after Hudson promised them warmer waters and fewer storms. They put in to the Faroe Islands, west of Norway, for provisions, and then set out across the Atlantic Ocean.

This 1898 print by artist Edward Moran depicts Native Americans watching from the shore of the Hudson River as the *Half Moon* gracefully sails its waters in September 1609.

If Hudson's crew had expected smoother sailing, they were mistaken. The *Half Moon* was struck by storm after storm on its way to the New World. By June 15, Juet reported in the ship's log, "We had a great storm, and [lost] overboard our foremast," taking the foresail with it. The passage continued the following day: "We were forced to try with our main sail," which, without the foresail, would have made controlling the ship even more difficult. It wasn't until June 19 that the weather grew calm enough for the crew to be able to improvise a temporary mast and foresail.

After that, presumably to everyone's relief, they had a stretch of calm weather. On June 25, Juet noted in his journal, "We had sight of a sail and gave . . . chase, but could not speak with her."

Even though Hudson's crew spotted another vessel, they couldn't catch up with it. Why they chased it might have been, despite Juet's lack of details, not merely an attempt to speak to another crew. They might have been attempting to capture what was probably a better ship, either for booty or to rid themselves of their own creaking vessel. (By 1609, it wasn't all that unlikely for a crew to spot another ship en route to the northern area of the New World. By that time, trade with the native people and a fishing and hunting industry were beginning—at least along the eastern coasts of what would later become Canada and the United States.)

By July 2, the *Half Moon* had safely reached what is now called the Grand Banks off Newfoundland's shore, and it sailed southwest. The crew constantly sounded for depth, which meant lowering a weighted cable, marked at regular intervals, so that they could tell the depth of the water and the conditions of the sea floor below them. The last thing Hudson would have wanted to do was run aground on a shoal (sandbar).

Soon the crew spied a fleet of French ships. But neither Hudson nor his crew spoke with any of them. This should not be a surprise: The French, after all, were commercial rivals of both the English and the Dutch.

Sea of Darkness

The *Half Moon* sailed on to Newfoundland, and from there, headed farther west and south. Less than two weeks later, they were within sight of land and described a shoreline, distinctive in its showy, white sandy beaches. They were off the coast of Nova Scotia and sailed on to what is now Penobscot Bay in Maine.

Meanwhile, the weather was foggy, occasionally so much so that the crew couldn't see where they were going and had to rely on constant sounding for depth. On July 13, they sailed blindly until the late afternoon, when they again saw land and the distant sails of other ships—presumably two more of the French fishing fleet. More fog later made visibility especially poor, so Hudson had the ship's anchors lowered, and the *Half Moon* sat, waiting patiently for clearer weather. Without much else to do, the men went fishing, and Juet commented joyfully about the great wealth of cod in the ocean waters.

Finally, to everyone's relief, the weather cleared again. And on July 17, Juet recounted two boats sailing out to meet them with six native people, all seemingly pleased at Hudson's arrival near the shore.

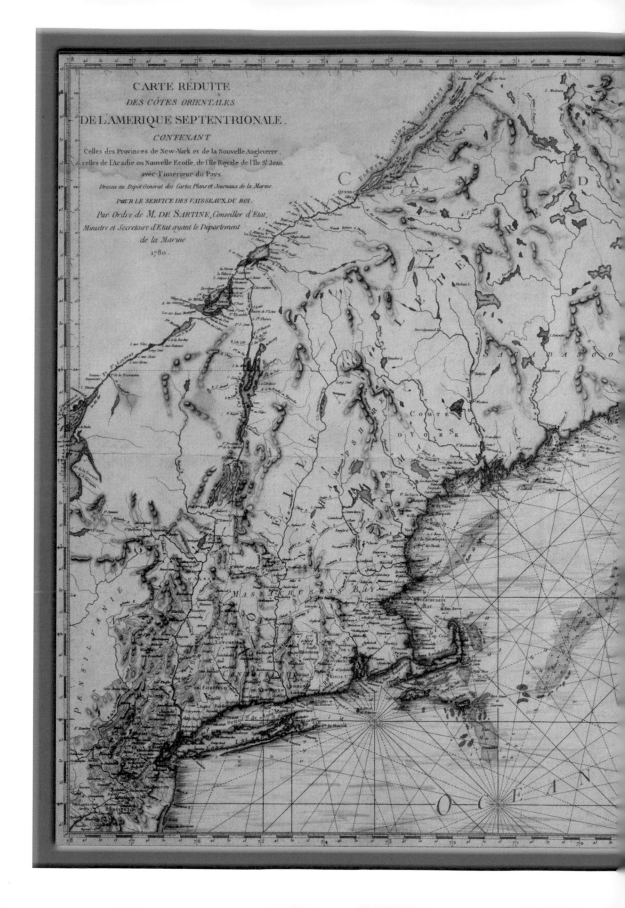

CARTE RÉDUITE
DES CÔTES ORIENTALES
DE L'AMERIQUE SEPTENTRIONALE.
CONTENANT
Celles des Provinces de New-York et de la Nouvelle Angleterre,
celles de l'Acadie ou Nouvelle Ecosse, de l'Ile Royale de l'Ile St. Jean
avec l'intérieur du Pays.
Dressée au Dépôt Général des Cartes, Plans et Journaux de la Marine
POUR LE SERVICE DES VAISSEAUX DU ROI,
Par Ordre de M. DE SARTINE, Conseiller d'Etat,
Ministre et Secretaire d'Etat ayant le Département
de la Marine
1780.

Henry Hudson became familiar with the ocean waters near Nova Scotia, as seen in this eighteenth-century French map, while sailing near its coast during the summer of 1609. His encounters with local Indians there were likely with members of Micmac tribes.

It wasn't surprising, since, as the crew soon learned, the native people had been trading peacefully with the French. Juet recalled that one of them spoke some French words. They had no reason to be alarmed by the sight of more Europeans. Juet described that meeting further. Hudson's crew gave the native people small gifts, and together they ate and drank with the European crew, telling tales of gold, silver, and copper mines that could be found nearby. This was far from wise, but the natives had no way of knowing their potential danger.

Hudson and his men, though, felt secure enough to go ashore—Henry Hudson's first foot-steps on the soil of the New World. Did he feel a thrill, or was he still too concerned with the hunt for that elusive Northwest Passage? Juet's journal gives us no clues.

5

THE NEW WORLD

---

*Our men went on land there, and saw great store of men,
women and children, who gave them tobacco at their coming
on land. So they went up into the woods, and saw great store
of goodly oaks and some currants. One of [the native persons]
came aboard and brought some dried [currants], and gave me
some, which were sweet and good. Some women also came to
us. They had copper tobacco pipes, and other things of copper
they did wear about their necks. At night they went on land
again, so we rode very quiet, but dared not trust them.*

—Excerpt from the journal of Robert Juet,
while aboard the *Half Moon,* 1609

Still recovering from their long journey, the
crew of the *Half Moon* refilled the ship's
casks with freshwater, worked on a replace-
ment mast cut from local timber, and caught a
total of thirty-one lobsters. Hudson even joined
the grand lobster feast, to which he also contributed two precious bottles of wine from his
small, private supply.

But Juet, for one, didn't let his guard down. He recorded in his journal that the local people came aboard the *Half Moon* once again and were friendly. Still, however, he questioned their behavior, but gives no reason for his mistrust. Was it wariness, or just his usual ill humor?

Juet continued, "Then we spied two French shallops [small boats] full of the country people come into the harbor. But they offered us no wrong, seeing we stood upon our guard. They brought many beaver skins and other fine furs, for which they would have changed [traded] for red gowns. For the French trade with them for red cassocks, knives, hatchets, copper, kettles . . . and other trifles."

Trouble Ahead

This early friendship of the local peoples with the French would have an echo a hundred years later during the French and Indian War, when the descendants of these natives sided with the French against the British colonists.

Information about the life and even the likeness of Henry Hudson has been sporadic and unreliable. There are few portraits of the explorer; all appeared after his death, and many historians are uncertain of their accuracy. Though many publications about his voyages were published during the seventeenth century, little to no information about the explorer himself was included. More than two centuries would pass before there was renewed interest in his accomplishments. In 1809, the New-York Historical Society commemorated the 200th anniversary of his "discovery" of New York.

But things were not going well between the native peoples and the crew of the *Half Moon*, although we can only guess at what might have been causing the trouble. On July 24, Juet noted that he and the entire crew continued to keep watch because they feared the native people's intentions. Days later, it seemed the brewing trouble burst into action.

"In the morning," Juet recorded, "we manned our scute with four muskets and six men, and took one of their shallops and brought it aboard. Then we manned our boat and scute with twelve men and muskets, and two stone pieces, or murderers [small cannons]. [We] drove the savages from their houses and took the spoil of them, as they would have done us."

Was there any justification for this action? Was there, as Juet seemed to claim, a plot forming against Hudson and his men? We will never have the exact answer to these questions, since the only account we have of what happened is that of the undeniably biased Juet. Hudson and his crew hoisted anchor and set sail again early on the morning of July 26.

Hudson is pictured here trading furs with local Native American tribes on the deck of the Half Moon. It wouldn't be long, however, before the Europeans and Indian tribes became distrustful of one another. This is partly because twelve members of Hudson's crew drove the Native Americans from their lands and stole their possessions.

While Hudson may not have been the first European to sight Manna-hatta (Manhattan Island), historians believe that he was very impressed with the lands there, calling them "the finest for cultivation that I ever in my life set foot upon." Years later, most historians literally translate the name Manna-hatta to mean "hilly island."

By August 3, the *Half Moon* had sailed past what is now Cape Cod. Hudson had a brief moment of disappointment: Seven years before him, another captain had actually claimed what Hudson thought was new land in 1602, a place he wanted to name "New Holland." But Hudson continued, and later had the satisfaction of being the first European to explore what is now Delaware Bay.

On August 4, the crew heard human voices from the shore and sent a boat to them, thinking that these might be European castaways. But they turned out to be native people, and this time, the encounter was a friendly one. They seemed genuinely happy to see the *Half Moon*'s crew. Juet wrote kindly of the encounter, recounting that the crew shared a meal with a man whom they soon sent back to land on one of Hudson's small boats.

The native man returned the favor by pointing out a river filled with lively fish. Juet and the rest of the crew observed the natives' tobacco pipes of red copper. With uncharacteristic charm, Juet was convinced of the land's bounty. (Sir John Hawkins, an English admiral and contemporary of Sir Francis Drake's, had first introduced England to the tobacco plant around 1565, but it was brought over from the New World to Europe as early as 1492.)

They sailed on for the rest of August, first down to the warm South, then back north again, never finding what was still driving Hudson's obsession—the elusive passage to Asia.

PETVN

Robert Juet, who wrote about the exploration of New York's Hudson Bay in the Half Moon's log, noted that the native inhabitants seemed "very glad of our coming, and brought green Tabacco, and gave us for it Knives and Beads," as documented in Gotham: A History of New York City to 1898 by Edwin G. Burrows and Mike Wallace. The tobacco plant in the print shown here was used as both medicine and food by the Indians.

By September, the *Half Moon* had reached what is now Lower New York Bay, anchoring near modern day Sandy Hook, New Jersey. Chances are that Hudson and his crew were pleased with the sights and condition of the land. Juet recorded in the ship's log that the terrain was good enough to settle, certainly bountiful, and able to sustain a larger population. He was even taken with the landscape and called it pleasant. As they lowered anchor, they came upon native people, members of a branch of the Algonquian group of Indian tribes. Hudson was probably relieved to see that they were friendly. The group greeted Hudson and his crew and exchanged native tobacco leaves for some of the *Half Moon*'s knives and other trinkets. Among the new foods Hudson tasted was corn. Not knowing what type of plant it was, he called it Turkish wheat. Later, Juet began referring to it as Indian wheat. Juet, predictably, remained ill at ease.

Attacked

As it turned out, Juet wasn't wrong about being wary. Hudson sent five of his men, led by John Colman, who'd been with Hudson on his first voyage, to explore another river. But as the five men sailed upriver, native warriors attacked them without warning. Colman was slain instantly by an arrow through the throat, while two other men in the group were wounded.

The survivors fled downriver, where they spent a terrifying night, unable to find the *Half Moon* in the darkness.

In the morning they recovered, and Colman's body was buried. The *Half Moon* remained at anchor through the night, and Hudson ordered a careful watch kept. But there was no further sign of trouble. To Hudson and the rest of the crew, it was plain enough: All the native people were now suspect.

Other local people came to trade with the *Half Moon* the following day, September 8, as though nothing had happened. Juet wrote about the dealings, which made no mention of Colman or the fact that he had been killed two days before.

But Hudson and his crew were still worried. On September 9, matters came to a head. Juet wrote that two canoes full of men met the *Half Moon*, each with his bow and arrow showing, while others held knives. Subsequently, two Native American men were taken as hostages by the English crew.

Unfortunately for Hudson, both hostages escaped. Hudson, who wrote in his journal, "Had they indicated by a cunning light in their eyes that they had knowledge of the foul murder, I was prepared . . . to exterminate all." He ordered the *Half Moon* moved to a safer distance inside the bay—now Upper New York Bay, or New York Harbor—anchoring overnight near the tip of the island now known as Manhattan.

During his third voyage Hudson encountered Native Americans from what is now New York and New Jersey. Although he and his crew greatly distrusted them, the Indians more than once brought Hudson and his crew food, tobacco, and fresh water.

But the native people followed. On the morning of September 12, twenty-eight canoes paddled out to meet the *Half Moon*. The ever-wary Juet wrote in the log that they were full of native people—men, women, and children—all intending to attack the English crew. Juet didn't realize that it would have been unlikely that warriors would take women and children with them to institute a conflict. Although the native people weren't allowed on board, they still managed to sell the crew some oysters and beans. In return for their trouble, Hudson took two of them hostage.

Hudson's Obsession Continues

The canoes departed by midday, and Hudson then ordered his crew to continue sailing north, up into the wide tidal river that now bears his name. Although Italian and Portuguese explorers had explored the river's mouth before; no one had yet explored the river itself, which spans two miles at its widest point. Hudson proudly claimed the entire region—now known as the Hudson River Valley—for his employers, the Dutch East India Company.

By the time the *Half Moon* had reached what is now Yonkers, Hudson had become hopeful that this, at last, was the passage to Asia. Considering the river's length and width, it's easy to see why he thought he had finally found the Northwest Passage. By September 15, the ship had reached the widest point of the Hudson (near where the Tappan Zee Bridge crosses it today), and it appeared to be a promising course to Arctic waters. Soon after, however, it began to narrow again and grow shallower. By the time they had reached what would one day be Albany, there was no longer any doubt that this was merely another river.

Adding to Hudson's discouragement, the two hostages escaped the following day, September 15, slipping through a porthole and swimming ashore, then yelling taunts back at the *Half Moon* and its crew. But that night, things

73

grew a little brighter. Juet recounted meeting other native people without wariness, individuals who intended no harm to the English crew.

By September 17, Hudson proved to himself without doubt that he had not, in fact, located a northern passage to Asia: The river grew so shallow that the *Half Moon* ran aground. Fortunately, since the Hudson is a tidal river (a waterway that allows the entrance of seawater to mix with fresh, unsalted waters), high tide was just enough to float the vessel free again. As far as the native people were concerned, it seemed as though Hudson and his crew had finally established a mutual level of trust between them.

"[Me and my first mate] determined to try some of the chief men of the country [to see] whether they had any treachery in them," Hudson wrote in his journal, as published in Thomas Janvier's book *Henry Hudson*. "So they took them down into the cabin [of the *Half Moon*], and gave them so much wine . . . that they were all merry. One of them had his wife with them, [who] sat so modestly as any of our country women would do in a strange place. In the end, one of them was drunk . . . and that was strange to them."

The man who'd gotten drunk slept the night aboard the *Half Moon*, and in the morning, he was returned to his people, who were as relieved to see him unharmed as Hudson and his men must have been to see their lack of hostility. But good humor soon fled Hudson, for he had to accept that there was no chance of sailing any farther north. At last, the *Half Moon* had to turn back.

Revenge

But trouble found them again. By October, more native people boarded the ship, and examined it and the crew's weapons. All seemed well, but soon one lingering man in a canoe, who was hanging about listlessly, slipped silently on board and attempted to steal some clothing and weapons. He was surprised by the first mate, who abruptly shot and killed him. Another man tried to climb into the boat too, but the ship's cook killed him as well, this time with a sword. Hudson hurriedly ordered the anchor raised, and the *Half Moon* sailed downriver.

By the next day, the *Half Moon* had gone twenty miles south. As the ship neared the island of Manhattan, canoes bearing at least a hundred angry warriors ambushed it. Arrows whizzed through the air, and shots rang out from the *Half Moon*. In the end, the vessel got away without the loss of English lives, but several of the native warriors died.

Hudson had had enough of this strange land and his inability to understand its people. The *Half Moon* returned to Europe in

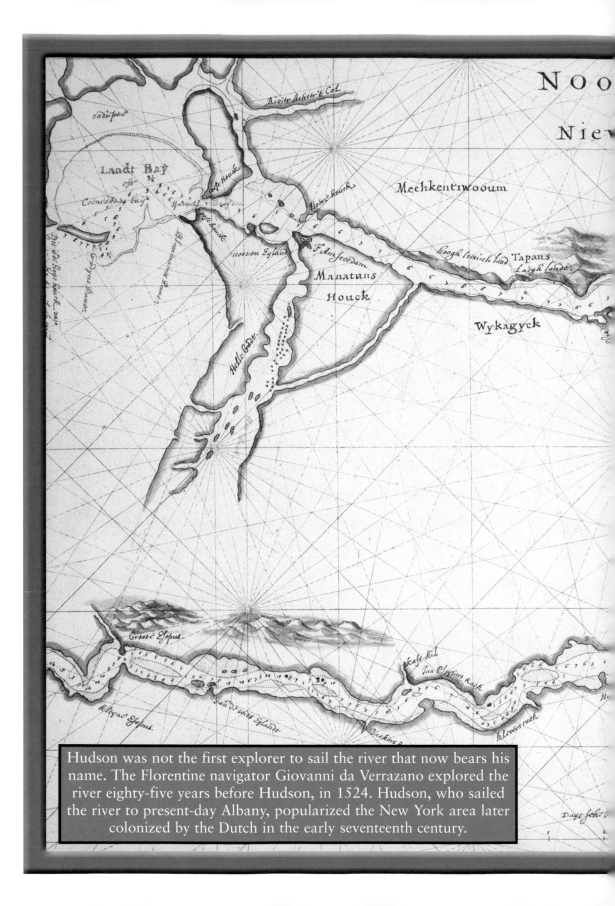

Hudson was not the first explorer to sail the river that now bears his name. The Florentine navigator Giovanni da Verrazano explored the river eighty-five years before Hudson, in 1524. Hudson, who sailed the river to present-day Albany, popularized the New York area later colonized by the Dutch in the early seventeenth century.

T RIVIER
in
eerlandt.

Weckae

Soy Luiakiers rack

Cogin than Negilandt

Cock rack

Paehami

Jan Brouwers hoek

Boffrack

Palchets Eyland

richanchong Ez

vighhoek

Langorick

Waranawankong's

elyne Eylo

oaftrich oft

Mahiecans

Biters Eylandt
Dry Eylanv

Smacks Eyland

Castele Eyland
Castrels Eyland
F. Orange

Mahiecans

valfich ovz

MAHIE CANS

Kilder houck

oor Een Grade.

3   4   5

November—oddly, docking first in England, not the Netherlands. This decision would anger Hudson's employers, who ordered that he return to them immediately afterward. Once Hudson had docked in London, he sent a letter to the Dutch East India Company, stating that he had not given up on the hunt for the Northwest Passage, and that he recommended a different voyage begin in spring of 1610.

The Dutch East India Company, understandably, demanded that he first bring the *Half Moon* back to them. But Hudson couldn't do it. He'd been notified by the English authorities in a letter of accusation of "voyaging to the detriment of his company," in other words, for working to profit a foreign power.

In December 1609, Henry Hudson was placed under arrest.

6

MUTINY

Wilson the boatswain and Henry Greene came to me . . . in my cabin and told me that they and the rest of their associates would . . . turn the master [Henry Hudson] and all the sick men into the shallop, and let them shift [assume responsibility] for themselves. For there was not fourteen days [food] left for all the company. Greene [said] . . . he would rather be hanged at home than starved abroad.

—From the journal of Robert Juet, 1611

Why was Henry Hudson arrested? Other Englishmen had worked for foreign countries before and not been punished. Some people wondered if he'd been spying. Others thought that this was simply a case of rival captains trying to get rid of him.

At any rate, Hudson's imprisonment, which turned out to be on a minor charge, didn't last very long. In fact, not only was he set free just days later, he made a deal with another company, the English East India Company, a

direct rival of his previous employers. His mission was to search yet again for the Northwest Passage and, not incidentally, for any gold or other valuable minerals along the way. One could only guess that Hudson must have been an incredibly convincing speaker to go from being perceived as a lawbreaker to an explorer on the verge of a major discovery. His next chance to search for the Northwest Passage would be as captain of the English ship *Discovery*. It was a sturdy vessel, larger and in better shape than his previous commands. (The *Half Moon* had been returned to the Dutch and sunk not long after.)

The Fourth Voyage

On April 17, 1610, the *Discovery* set sail with a crew of twenty-two men that again included Hudson's son John and the still bitter-minded Juet. For this fourth voyage, only a partial account from Hudson remains, but a more complete account was kept by another member of the fateful crew, Abacuk Prickett.

While historians have long known that Henry Hudson couldn't suppress the mutiny on board the Discovery in 1611, they suspect the troubles stemmed from various sources, including Hudson's inability to resolve differences between himself and his crew. His men, then starving, also believed that Hudson was hoarding food in his private cabin, later claiming that they had found a stash there of hardtack, wine, and other goods after forcing the explorer off his own ship with several of the sicker crew members as well as his son John.

Hudson, still in English waters, stated in his journal on April 22 that he put one of the crew, a Master Coleburne, off the ship in a pinkie (small boat) bound for London, while moored at Lee. This may have been because he was a company man, there to keep an eye on the English East India Company's investment. Hudson wouldn't have wanted someone watching his every move. To replace him, and without telling his employers, Hudson took on Henry Greene at Gravesend, a man he had known in London. Unfortunately, Hudson may not have known that Greene also had a reputation as a gambler and troublemaker.

But there was little trouble through the month of May. The crew sighted Iceland by May 11 and witnessed the eruption of the Icelandic volcano Mount Hekla. While Hudson didn't mention it, Prickett recounted the lively event in his journal, writing how the crew saw the famous hill casting out a great fire, a sign that he believed would certainly bring bad weather for the journey.

Tensions Mount

This also marked the beginning of trouble aboard the *Discovery*. A few days afterward, Henry Greene argued with Edward Wilson, the ship's surgeon, which turned into an actual fistfight. Hudson broke it up, taking Greene's side, while the crew sided with Wilson. There were uneasy

Abacuk Prickett, who also wrote the account of Hudson's last voyage, recorded the eruption of Mount Hekla, the Icelandic volcano pictured here. Prickett was certain that the eruption was a sign of bad omens to come, or at the very least a condition that would contribute to bad weather.

feelings all around, although Hudson presumably did what he could to soothe everyone. Later, he wrote in his journal that Wilson "had a tongue that would wrong his best friend."

The crew disagreed. Juet, for one, was certain that Hudson had wanted Greene on board for one reason only—as his spy to keep him posted on what the crew was saying. Hudson, when he heard this, was so furious that he wanted to put Juet off the ship at once, but he was convinced by the others that they needed Juet's skills.

About the only pleasant part of their voyage past Iceland was the chance the men had to bathe in one of the island's geothermal pools, which, as Prickett noted in his journal, had waters that were hot enough to scorch the region's fowl. The hot water would have felt wonderful to men who'd just been sailing over icy seas.

By June 1, the *Discovery* was on its way to Greenland. But when they reached it three days later, Hudson and his crew found there was too much ice to let them draw close. Instead, Hudson headed the *Discovery* southwest until there was some clear sailing up to the northwest again on June 15. But it wasn't completely clear.

The *Discovery* had a narrow run-in with a pod of whales. Prickett described in the ship's log what could have been a disaster. At least three whales came so close to the ship they could hardly be avoided. One whale even passed under the vessel, causing greater alarm. The *Discovery* could very well have been overturned by something as large as a whale if the animal had surfaced just then, but Prickett added that the stability of the vessel had returned to normal in the frigid waters.

This 1826 map of North America, created by Joseph Perkins, includes the United States, Mexico, Central America, and Rupert's Land. Held by the Hudson Bay Company from 1670 to 1870, Rupert's Land was sold to Canada in 1870 for 300,000 pounds sterling.

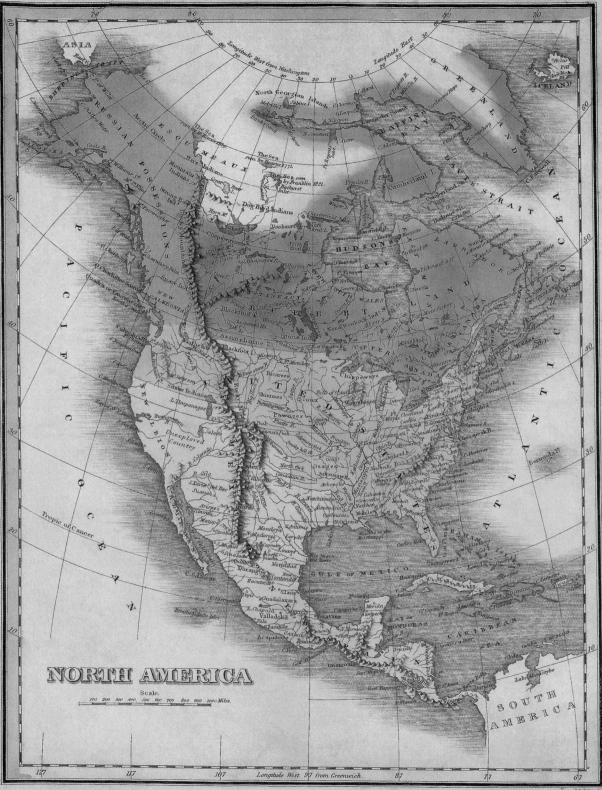

NORTH AMERICA

Scale.

100 200 300 400 500 600 700 800 900 1000 Miles.

Great Islands of Ice

By June 21, the *Discovery* had reached what is now the coast of Labrador, but again it ran into ice. For three days, the sailing was slow, though they did catch a glimpse of Resolution Island on June 24, but just as swiftly they lost sight of it. Hudson ordered them to continue sailing due west.

Four days later, the *Discovery* reached what is now called Hudson Strait, part of Canada, between northern Quebec Province and Baffin Island. But there was ice as far as the eye could see. Hudson had no way of knowing that the strait was dangerous because of icebergs until the middle of July. Instead, the *Discovery*, pressed by winds, was again forced south, blocked by ice from getting near any shore.

By the beginning of July, Prickett noted in his journal, "Some of our men . . . fell sick. I will not say it was for fear, though I saw small signs of other grief." By this, he meant that discontent was rising among the crew. Hudson, however, seemed not to have noticed, since he wrote nothing about it.

He did notice that on July 6 and 7, there seemed to be ice blocking them from ever sailing farther west. The *Discovery* sailed into a bay but got nowhere. Prickett painted a dramatic picture in his journal.

"Into the current we went, and made our way [north by northwest] till we met with ice. Wherefore our master . . . cleared

86

himself of this ice and stood [steered] to the south, then the west, through store of floating ice. We gained a clear sea . . . till we met with more ice, first with great islands, then with store of the smaller sort. Between them, we made our course northwest, till we met with ice again. We saw one of the great islands of ice overturn, which was a good warning to us . . . The next day we had a storm, and the wind brought the ice fast upon us. Our course was as the ice did lie, sometimes to the north, then to the northwest, then to the west, and then to the southwest, but still enclosed with ice. The more [Hudson] strove, the worse he was."

The Hudson Bay Company

The Hudson's Bay Company later explored the North American and Canadian region and set up quite a trading empire in the eighteenth and nineteenth centuries. The company still exists. A full-scale replica of its sailing ship Nonsuch was built and sailed the coast of England, the Great Lakes, and the Pacific Northwest before being assigned a permanent home in the Manitoba Museum of Man and Nature in Winnipeg, Canada. Hudson Bay blankets made of heavy wool can still be bought from Canada, and the company runs a Canadian chain of department stores called simply the Bay.

In 1602 a number of small, independent trading companies, all operating out of the Netherlands, formed a coalition known as the "Verenigde Oostindische Compagnie," now called the Dutch East India Company. Its purpose was to promote trade with Asia. The government of the Netherlands gave the new company extensive powers to help it achieve its goal, including the right to enter into treaties, to maintain military forces, and to produce coinage.

By this time, even Hudson was in despair. He confessed to Prickett that he was certain they were never going to get out of the ice and that they would die there.

The crew, understandably, wasn't any happier. They probably would have mutinied then and there if that would have gotten them home. But Hudson, who might have been unable to think of anything else to say, proudly displayed his charts to show the crew that they had sailed farther west than any Englishmen ever had before. He left the choice to them: Should they continue or not?

This, again, wasn't wise, since what the crew must have wanted most was a strong leader. Instead, they split, half wanting to go home, the other half willing to continue. And others were, as Prickett wrote in his journal, merely desperate to get out of the ice and head south. Many of them, Prickett added ominously, said words that would be remembered later.

At any rate, there was no real choice then but to work the ship free of ice. At last they managed to maneuver the *Discovery* loose, and Hudson insisted on continuing the journey.

In the days that followed, from July 8 until the end of the month, the *Discovery* continued west and followed a pattern of avoiding icebergs, anchoring to ride out storms, and exploring island after barren island. Once, the men attempted to shoot a polar bear, but it escaped over the loose ice floes. The *Discovery* was nearly caught in what is now Ungava Bay in Canada, but the crew managed to edge their way along the shore of the bay and out into open sea again, this time headed northwest. Hudson mapped and named all the islands they found, usually after English royalty, but by this point, the crew probably didn't care what he named them.

Then, at the beginning of August, Hudson wrote that they had finally sailed into a great expanse of water. He and his crew had entered what is now Hudson Bay.

Hudson wasn't ready to give up. This was a bay, but soon the *Discovery* came across a deep inlet flowing into the sea from the northwest. Hudson ordered the crew to sail into it.

Along the way, they stopped on an island covered with nesting seabirds and remarked about its beautiful grasses and rounded hills of stone, which they believed were made by the hands of Christians. What they had really found were some Inuit cairns being used to cure duck meat.

Hudson was in no mood for dallying, even though Prickett, among others, asked for more time, a day or two, to recover in this unexpectedly pleasant place. But Hudson insisted that they all return to the *Discovery* at once. Prickett noted in his journal that Hudson refused to remain there, still obsessed by his mission.

This was another mistake on Hudson's part. His men would have been a great deal more agreeable to his ideas if he had allowed them the brief vacation. By now, Hudson's mistakes were adding up to a disagreeable crew.

A Sealed Fate

The *Discovery* continued exploring islands. The crew took to arguing among themselves, and finally with Hudson, over what direction to take. At last, on September 10, matters came to a head for the first, but not the last, time. Sour-tongued Juet got into a battle of words with his captain, and Hudson had definitely had enough. Hudson ordered a shipboard trial of Juet for mutiny. We have the account written in the ship's log by crewmember Thomas Woodhouse, who described how Hudson let Juet speak for himself. "There were proved so many and great abuses, and mutinous matters" that Juet had raised that "it was fit time to punish and cut off farther occasions of the like mutinies," according to the account in the log.

Juet was promptly demoted and replaced. Then Hudson added that if the other "offenders yet behaved themselves henceforth honestly . . . he would forget injuries."

He might, but would they?

Things quickly worsened. The *Discovery* spent the month of October aimlessly wandering through Hudson Bay, going northwest, north and then south again, and finally east. It was as though Hudson had finally given up on finding what he sought. And by the end of October, there was no doubt in his mind that they were going to have to settle down for the winter. The crew managed to haul the ship aground, and they did what they could to survive the dark and freezing cold of the subarctic temperatures. Prickett wrote in his journal, "To speak of all our trouble would be too tedious."

Hudson seemed to have lost control, getting into arguments with the crew over matters he should have been able to settle. In one case, he gave a dead crewman's cloak to another crewman instead of following the custom of auctioning it off to provide the dead man's next of kin with some money. Hudson also shouted at men over small matters using foul, even profane, language. And he fought with the man he had brought aboard, treacherous Henry Greene, who, as Prickett wrote, attempted to discredit and humiliate his position as captain.

A tragic fate awaits both Hudson and his teenage son John, both depicted in this 1881 painting by John Collier. Their tiny lifeboat was marooned in icy waters on a cold night in 1611. Hudson, along with six loyal crewmen, some sickened with disease and all certainly starving, must have known they had no chance of survival before they disappeared.

Until the end of November, the men were able to catch and kill enough birds to keep them alive. But then the birds went south, and the crew was reduced to eating frogs and even moss, and treating scurvy—a disease brought about by vitamin C deficiency—with a natural medicine. There was a visit from one local tribesman, but after a brief meeting with the desperate Hudson, the man left and never returned.

Horror

As the winter turned slowly into spring, the men were able to catch about 500 small fish and rejoiced. But that many fish would not be found again. By the middle of May 1611, Greene had convinced some to leave the *Discovery* and fend for themselves, but they were dismayed when they ran into a hostile tribe who set the forest on fire before they could make any approach.

At last the brief northern spring warmed the waters enough so that the *Discovery* could be relaunched. Hudson, weeping, doled out what remained of the crew's food and water. There should, according to the listing, have been nine cheeses on board, but Hudson showed only five. Greene promptly claimed that he was holding back provisions. Hudson retorted that the remaining foods were spoiled, far too much for eating.

Hudson is cast adrift after the mutiny on the Discovery. Two legends survive concerning Hudson's fate. One tells of an Inuit band that found a boat filled with dead white men, and a single survivor, a white boy—was it John Hudson? Nothing more is known of his fate. A legend in the Ottawa Valley of Ontario, Canada, tells that Hudson, his son, and his abandoned crew were captured by natives and enslaved, then led on a trip down the Ottawa River before they were killed. Today there are stories of "HH" markings on rocks along the banks of the Ottawa River, but these legends cannot be confirmed.

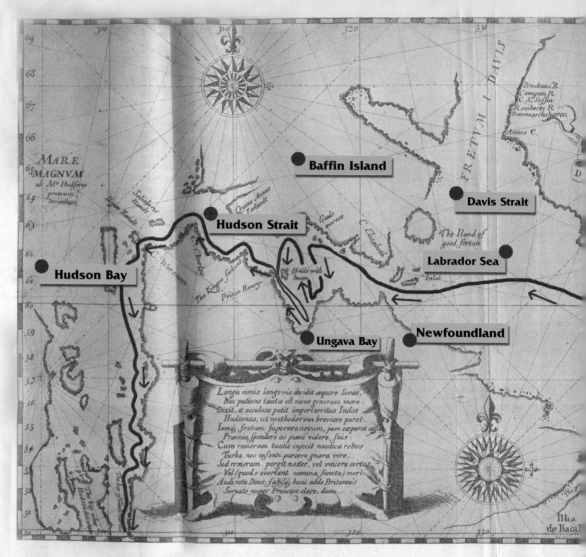

Chart of 1612, Engraved after Hudson's Own Maps and N

This is the first known map of Hudson's northern discoveries. It was published in Amsterdam, the Netherlands, in 1612. Because he had sailed for the Dutch, the citizens there became greatly interested in Hudson's accomplishments after hearing the news that the explorer was missing.

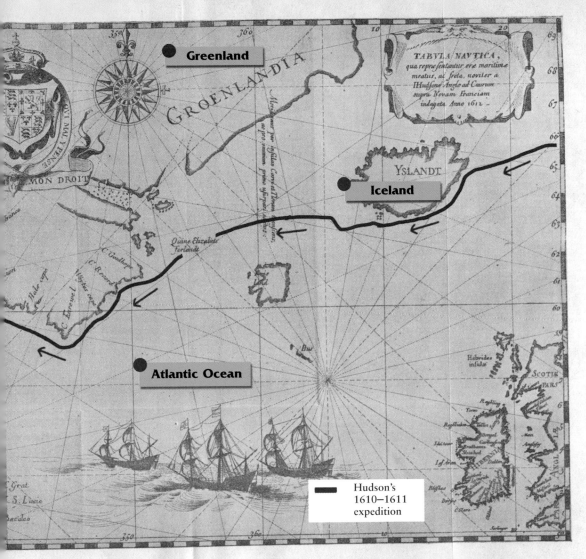

TABVLA NAVTICA,
qua repræsentuntur oræ maritimæ
meatus, ac freta, noviter a
IHudsono Anglo ad Caurum
supra Novam Franciam
indagata Anno 1612 –

Greenland

GROENLANDIA

Iceland

YSLANDT

Atlantic Ocean

▬▬▬ Hudson's
1610–1611
expedition

ons, Showing Particularly the Course of his Explorations in 1610

On May 18, to everyone's horror, the ship was caught again in the ice, and the entire crew was certain that they were doomed. But the ice released the *Discovery* on May 20. The crew was certain that they were finally going home. But Hudson instead ordered the ship to be sailed west instead, and he even went so far as to have the crew's gear searched for hoarded bread.

That was his final mistake.

On May 22, the mutiny began. Led by Henry Greene, with Juet assisting, the mutineers seized Hudson, his son, and approximately six other sickly crew members who still supported him, cast them off the *Discovery* into a small boat, and abandoned them.

Hudson's voyage of exploration was suddenly over. The *Discovery* sailed off, and soon the small boat was lost in the distance.

That was the last anyone ever saw of the explorer Henry Hudson.

Most of the mutineers, including Juet, died on the long journey back to England. In September, only six men remained, and they were rescued by a fishing boat. They had been away from England for nearly a year and a half.

In October, the mutineers were questioned, but a formal trial was postponed until 1618. By then, those who survived after so long were found not guilty and went free.

This Hudson family coat of arms was most likely centuries old by the time Henry Hudson was born. Its ornamental red flower pattern, combined with a black cross, could have indicated that the Hudsons were Christian. Coats of arms indicated the heraldic (official genealogical insignia) bearings of the wearer or his achievements. They originated in the fourteenth century and were commonly embroidered garments worn over armor.

Katherine Hudson did her best to persuade the Dutch East India Company to send out a rescue party for her husband. It took her three long years, but at last they sent out a ship. It found no trace of the doomed explorer.

Katherine was now officially widowed, and she sought compensation for the loss of her husband to the point where the company directors began referring to her as "that troublesome and impatient woman" in their records.

But she won the case. Katherine Hudson even forced the English East India Company to fund her journey to India, where she purchased indigo, a valuable dye. Showing a strong head for business she returned from her travels a wealthy woman who was even received at the royal court. She died in 1624, leaving everything to her two surviving sons, Richard and Oliver.

Henry Hudson has not been forgotten by history as his name can be found all over New York City and State, and in northeastern Canada.

Hudson is remembered not as the explorer who failed to find the Northwest Passage, but as an explorer whose discoveries completed the details of many modern maps.

CHRONOLOGY

1553 Sir Hugh Willoughby perishes while searching for the northern passage to Asia.

1555 The Muscovy Company is formed to establish trade with Russia.

1556 Stephen Burrough navigates to the entrance of the Kara Sea.

1558 Queen Elizabeth I comes into power.

1576 Martin Frobisher sails north through Frobisher Bay and reaches Baffin Island.

1577 Sir Francis Drake circumnavigates the globe.

1582 Richard Hakluyt publishes his first book, *Diverse Voyages Touching the Discovery of America.*

1585   John Davis's first northern voyage.

1595   First Dutch voyage to the Far East.

1600   Hakluyt publishes *The Principal Navigations*.

1602   Formation of the Dutch East India Company.

1607   Founding of Jamestown by the Virginia Company.

1608   Henry Hudson searches for the Northwest Passage for the Dutch East India Company.

1609   Hudson explores present-day New York.

1610   Hudson explores Hudson Bay.

1611   Mutiny aboard the *Discovery*. Henry Hudson disappears after he is set adrift in a small boat.

1624   The Dutch settle Manhattan Island.

1631   Luke Foxe and Thomas James make the last attempt to find the Northwest Passage during the age of exploration.

GLOSSARY

astrolabe A medieval instrument used to determine the altitude of the sun or other celestial bodies.

cabin boy A boy servant aboard a ship.

carrack A type of merchant ship used between the fourteenth and sixteenth centuries; a galleon.

Cathay The ancient name for China.

cross staff An early sixteenth-century instrument for measuring the altitude of a heavenly body.

Elizabethan Era Relating to the time during the reign of England's Queen Elizabeth I (1558–1603).

hardtack A hard biscuit or bread made only with flour and water; sea bread; sea biscuit.

mutiny   Open rebellion against constituted authority.

Novaya Zemlya (Nova Zembla)   Islands situated off the northern coast of Russia.

prow   The forward part of a ship's hull; the bow.

quadrant   An early instrument for measuring altitude, consisting of a ninety-degree graduated arc with a moveable radius for measuring angles.

Renaissance   A time period in Europe between the fourteenth and seventeenth centuries that was marked by great advancements in the arts, sciences, and exploration.

scurvy   A disease caused by a deficiency of vitamin C with symptoms that include nausea, weakness, loss of hair and teeth, and eventually death. Scurvy was the most prevalent cause of death among sailors between the fifteenth and seventeenth centuries.

shallop   An open boat fitted with oars, sails, or both.

shoal A sandy elevation of the bottom of a body of water, constituting a hazard to navigation; a sandbank or sandbar.

steer To guide a vessel by means of a device such as a rudder, paddle, or wheel.

sterncastle A two-story cabin on a sailing vessel.

FOR MORE INFORMATION

The Elisha Kent Kane Historical Society
530 East 86th Street
New York, NY 10028
Web site: http://www.ekkane.org

The New York Historical Society
2 West 77th St.
New York, NY 10024
(212) 873-3400
Web site: http://www.nyhistory.org

Web Sites

Due to the changing nature of Internet links, the Rosen Publishing Group, Inc., has developed an online list of Web sites related to the subject of this book. This site is updated regularly. Please use this link to access the list:

http://www.rosenlinks.com/lee/hehu/

FOR FURTHER READING

Brown, Warren. *The Search for the Northwest Passage* (World Explorers). New York: Chelsea House Publishers, 1991.

Casson, Lionel. *An Illustrated History of Ships and Boats*. New York: Doubleday & Co., 1964.

Goodman, Joan Elizabeth. *Beyond the Sea of Ice: Voyages of Henry Hudson* (Great Explorers Book 1). New York: Mikaya Press, 1999.

Johnson, Donald S. *Charting the Sea of Darkness: The Four Voyages of Henry Hudson*. Tokyo and New York: Kodansha International, 1995.

Mattern, Joanne. *The Travels of Henry Hudson* (Explorers and Exploration). Austin, TX: Raintree/Steck-Vaughn Publishers, 2000.

Weiner, Eric. *The Story of Henry Hudson, Master Explorer*. New York: Dell Publishing, 1991.

BIBLIOGRAPHY

Gillmer, Thomas C. *A History of Working Watercraft of the Western World*. Camden, ME: International Marine, 1994.

Hale, John R. *Age of Exploration (The Great Ages of Man)*. New York: Time-Life Books, 1966.

Hornell, James. *Water Transport: Origins and Early Evolution*. Boston, MA: Cambridge University Press, 1946.

Janvier, Thomas A. *Henry Hudson: A Brief Statement of His Aims and His Achievements. To Which Is Added a Newly-Discovered Partial Record Now First Published of The Trial of the Mutineers by Whom He and Others Were Abandoned to Their Death*. New York and London: Harper & Brothers Publishers, 1909.

Morison, Samuel Eliot. *The European Discovery of America, Volumes One and Two*. New York: Oxford University Press, 1986.

Mulligan, Tim. *The Hudson River Valley: A History and Guide*. New York: Random House, Inc., 1981.

Read, John M. Jr. *A Historical Inquiry Concerning Henry Hudson, His Friends, Relatives, and Early Life*. Albany, NY: Joel Munsell, 1866.

INDEX

About the Author

Josepha Sherman is a professional author and folklorist, with more than 40 books and 125 short stories and articles in print. She is an active member of the Authors Guild and the Science Fiction Writers of America. Her Web site may be viewed at http://www.josephasherman.com.

Photo Credits

Series Design

Tahara Hasan

Editor

Joann Jovinelly